WINDOWS OF WORSHIP™

REAL LIFE REFLECTIONS

Shining His Light

PAUL S. WILLIAMS, *Editor*

Stories for Spiritual Growth

Standard
PUBLISHING
Bringing The Word to Life™

Published by Standard Publishing, Cincinnati, Ohio. A division of
Standex International Corporation. Printed in China.

Edited by: Paul S. Williams
Content editor: Molly Detweiler
Art direction and design: Rule29
Cover design: Rule29 | rule29.com

ISBN 0-7847-1661-7

11 10 09 08 07 06 05   9 8 7 6 5 4 3 2 1

He made it simple . . .

God didn't give us 10,000 different rules to follow. We don't even have to worry about the 613 laws of the Old Testament—set out for a different age. No, as Christians we have just one responsibility. To live like Christ, reflecting him in our lives. I said he made it simple. I did not say it was easy!

So how do we do it? Jesus' answer was simple: Love God with all your heart, soul, and mind, and love your neighbor as yourself.

That is our challenge, to love God with everything we have, and to love our neighbors likewise. My hope is that, as you read these reflections from the lives of people who have answered that challenge, you will be encouraged to do the same. Keep it simple: live a real life, reflecting a very real God.

PAUL S. WILLIAMS
Chairman of the Board of Stewards
The Christian Network, Inc.

Let us fix our eyes on Jesus, the author and perfecter of our faith,
who for the joy set before him endured the cross, scorning its
shame, and sat down at the right hand of the throne of God.

HEBrews 12:2

Into Their Eyes

My outlook on life is constantly changing. Events change me—events like the attacks of September 11 and the wars in Afghanistan and Iraq. But I find myself most changed by the people I encounter—people like Ron and Cami.

Ron and Cami are a wonderful couple in their early 40s, with three children, Tanner, Garrett, and Whitney. This family is changing me because of the

way they handle personal suffering. Several years
ago Cami had a radical mastectomy; and through
it, I watched her model complete trust in God's
provision and care. I looked straight into that
family's eyes and saw peace.

A few years later, Cami's blood tests revealed more
cancer—which meant chemotherapy, radiation, and
hair loss. But it did not mean a loss of faith. Instead,
I looked into Cami's eyes and saw joy.

Just recently routine tests indicated more cancer.
Ron told me the liver was involved this time, and
the prognosis isn't good. But I looked into his eyes
and saw a steadfast faith—one that continues to
change me.

If you were to meet Ron and Cami, you would see
two tired people. They are tired of tests. Tired of
medicine. Tired of figuring out what to tell their

children. Tired of wanting to plan for a future that may never come. You could say they are running on empty.

But if you were to look into their eyes, behind the weariness, you would see that which is changing me. You would see peace and joy. How do they manage this tranquility when the future is defined by the next cancer test? The answer, my friend, is found in someone bigger than you and I. Ron and Cami have chosen to trust God. Though Cami is in the midst of a terrible cloud with no silver lining, Ron and Cami still trust God.

This life has more questions than answers. But when the fumes in your gas tank have run out, and your wheels stop moving, you still will have a decision to make. Do you give up, or do you trust the one who specializes in bringing peace and comfort to those in pain?

When Jesus' disciples were confused and discouraged, Jesus asked them if they would leave him. Peter, through his pain, answered: "Lord, to whom shall we go? You have the words of eternal life" (John 6:68). No matter how bad things got, no one could take that from him, and he was willing to stake his life on it. Jesus had the words of eternal life.

And in that sentence is Ron and Cami's answer—my answer, and the answer for all who so choose. Jesus does have words of eternal life. He can bring peace and joy in the midst of terrible pain. Ron and Cami will tell you there is no other choice. And you can see that they chose rightly, just by looking into their eyes.

■■ GREG ALLEN AND PAUL S. WILLIAMS

What events or people have changed your outlook? How are you different because of those circumstances or relationships?

What do others see in your eyes when you are going through a difficult time? Do you think your outlook on life has ever changed someone else's for the better? Why or why not?

Be still, and know that I am God.

PSALM 46:10

Productive Elevator Time

I recently read an article about the use of e-mail in the business environment of the twenty-first century. A CEO of a major corporation was thrilled that he had found a use for the "unproductive" time he spent riding the elevator—he fires up his PalmPilot® and reads and answers e-mail.

To quote the executive, "Finally, no more time wasted staring at the elevator doors."

Americans have become obsessed with productivity. Heaven forbid that we step away from our work for a few seconds while we're on an elevator. No. That's time to turn on your hand-held computer and answer your e-mail.

Wait a minute! Hold on! Now answer me just one question. How long can we keep this up?

I have a golden retriever. In the winter she can run a full seven miles with me without so much as a hiccup. In the summer, however, I'm lucky if she can go a mile and a quarter. It's just too hot for her.

But Lily knows how to take care of herself. When she's had enough, she just stops. Never mind that I keep tugging on her leash. She's done. She lies down in whatever yard we happen to be near and won't budge another inch. Lily knows when she's overheated.

I, on the other hand, seem to have no idea when I'm overheated. And I'm a part of an entire culture that seems to have the same problem. Where does the madness stop?

Jesus didn't live what you would call a leisurely life. He was up before dawn, with many an agonizing late night. But somehow he didn't get caught up in the race—he lived above it. While he was speaking to a first-century audience, Jesus had some pointed words to say about life in the twenty-first.

He said, "Therefore I tell you, do not worry about your life, what you will eat or drink; or about your body, what you will wear. Is not life more important than food, and the body more important than clothes? Look at the birds of the air; they do not sow or reap or store away in barns, and yet your heavenly Father feeds them. Are you not much more valuable than they? Who of you

by worrying can add a single hour to his life?"
(Matthew 6:25-27). You can't. It's that simple.
So stop playing the game.

When your life is over, no one is going to remember you because you learned how to make your
elevator time productive. If they remember you
fondly at all, it will be because you learned to love
and be loved. So go ahead and stare at those elevator doors, and do absolutely nothing. Take a deep
breath and let it out slowly, and be thankful that
God is in charge—not you.

PAUL S. WILLIAMS

How does your schedule look? Is it a healthy balance between being productive and allowing time to be still? Or are you overheating without realizing it? Look at your daily schedule and give it an honest evaluation.

Are there things that you can cut out of your schedule to allow more time for rest and being still in God's presence and reaching out to others with his love? Ask God to help you find ways to simplify and achieve the balance he wants for your life.

Praise be to the God and Father of our Lord Jesus Christ! In his great mercy he has given us new birth into a living hope through the resurrection of Jesus Christ from the dead, and into an inheritance that can never perish, spoil or fade.

1 PETER 1:3, 4

A Longfellow Life

A certain woman had the wild misfortune of being widowed seven times. At least that was the story a group of skeptics told Jesus. They asked, "Now then, at the resurrection, whose wife will she be of the seven, since all of them were married to her?" (Matthew 22:28).

They, of course, were not seeking an answer to their question. They were just trying to point out what they thought was an absurd idea—life after death. Those skeptics aren't alone in their doubts.

The poet Henry Wadsworth Longfellow wrote these words to a familiar Christmas carol:

> In despair I bowed my head;
> "There is no peace on earth," I said,
> "For hate is strong and mocks the song
> Of peace on earth, good will to men."

His own skepticism inspired those words.

Longfellow's doubts were as rooted in reality as was the beard on his face. Longfellow's full beard was not dictated by fashion as much as necessity. At the beginning of the Civil War, his wife was killed in a fire. He tried to extinguish the flames by wrapping himself around her. His face was so badly burned that shaving became impossible.

Three years later, Longfellow's oldest son, Charles, was severely wounded while fighting for the army of the Potomac. There was no end in sight—of the war, the grief, or the militant hatred.

Longfellow understood skepticism and despair. With the words of his poetry he was asking, "How can we, in the presence of so many dead, trust in a God of life?"

Jesus responded to the skeptics in his usual manner—by challenging their assumptions. The grave is not the final word.

"I am the resurrection and the life," Jesus said. "He who believes in me will live, even though he dies" (John 11:25).

Even in the midst of despair, Longfellow knew that truth. He wrote in his *Psalm of Life:*

Tell me not, in mournful numbers
Life is but an empty dream!—
For the soul is dead that slumbers
And things are not what they seem.
Life is real! Life is earnest!
And the grave is not its goal;
Dust thou art, to dust returnest
Was not spoken of the soul.

 ERIC SNYDER AND PAUL S. WILLIAMS

What things in life cause you to struggle with despair like the poet Longfellow? What verses bring you the most hope in the midst of your dark times?

Write your own psalm of life (it doesn't have to rhyme or even be spelled correctly), expressing your hope in Jesus as the resurrection and the life. Praise him from your heart for not leaving us in our despair!
Who can you share this hope with today?

As the deer pants for streams of water,
so my soul pants for you, O God.
My soul thirsts for God, for the living God.
When can I go and meet with God?

PSALM 42:1, 2

I Was Made for This

I met Ellen in New York City. Wounded by her father and always striving for his acceptance, Ellen was driven to succeed. She became a professional with a reputation as a hardworking up-and-comer. There was only one problem— Ellen's soul was empty.

Ellen kept herself busy, and most days she was able to keep the ache and longing in the distance.

But then came September 11, 2001, and Ellen was forced, as many New Yorkers were, to look beyond her day-to-day business and find a deeper thread running through her life. To her dismay, all she could find was her frantic and lonely longing for meaning —a longing that her six-figure income couldn't begin to answer. Ellen wanted to be loved with no strings attached. She wanted to know grace, mercy, and forgiveness, and feel their impact.

Ellen had become disillusioned with the church at an early age; but when pain is deep, a lost soul will look anywhere. So when Ellen's friend invited her to the worship service of a brand-new church, she took a deep breath, got out of bed, and walked into the Sunday morning services of a year-old congregation.

It was not what she expected. The music was inspiring. It drew her toward the God she wasn't even sure existed. A woman gave the Communion meditation, inviting all to the banquet table of Christ, and the minister spoke straight to the emptiness in Ellen's soul.

"Everything just felt right," she said, "like I was made for this."

Ellen was still skeptical, but she kept returning Sunday after Sunday. Slowly, the face of the one she worshiped came into focus through the eyes of those who sang and partook with her. They became her companions on the journey, with similar stories and a common life of worship.

I recently asked Ellen which element of that first Sunday touched her most. I was asking as a church-planting administrator. Fortunately, her answer went far deeper than just a helpful hint for new churches. Without hesitation she said, "The worship—the sense that I was created to do this—to worship somebody or something."

Some people enjoy high church services with incense and candles, robed priests and processionals. Others like contemporary worship with simple lyrics projected on overhead screens. Still others prefer hand-clapping, foot-stomping, camp meeting services. Which is best?

When the worship styles are tallied, and the verdict is in, I believe that what most of us are looking for on a Sunday morning is the sense that we were, in fact, created to worship and invited to the banquet table. And if we leave the church service with that deep sense of awe and peace, I don't think we really care whether it was a five-string banjo or a five-manual organ that got us there.

■■ PAUL S. WILLIAMS

What inspires you to worship?
What do you feel created to do?

What or who draws you closer to God? How?
What might you do to help others draw closer to the
Lord, just as someone did for Ellen?

Remember your word to your servant,
for you have given me hope.
My comfort in my suffering is this:
Your promise preserves my life.

PSALM 119:49, 50

Of Pain and Hope

I had been in pain for a long time. I did not find much redemptive value in the chronic nagging discomfort I had known for the better part of three years. It did not bring wisdom. It just hurt.

I had been to every practitioner in the suburbs of New York City. Finally, one of the specialists I saw sent me to Jeffrey John Ellis, a physical therapist. After a couple of months of treatment, he convinced my body to comply with his manipulative reminders, and my pain was gone. But there is more to the story.

Jeff was a faith-filled man. He had clear eyes and a good heart, and he heeded the clarion call from God—he was a refreshing soul on the flatlands of Long Island.

I had been through a long dark night—from physical pain, from the never-ending pressure of directing a sizable ministry, from having three teenagers in my house, and from working with people who were hurt and wounded spiritually. I was being drained on several fronts, and soon I found myself battling my own disillusionment with God.

That's when the physical therapist came into my life on the fresh breeze of the Holy Spirit. My spirit was renewed, and my soul was stirred.

My friend Jeff enjoyed his work as a church elder. A wonderful husband and father, he was also a nationally renowned teacher.

Then my friend Jeff was diagnosed with leukemia.

Jeff e-mailed me not three weeks after his diagnosis. He sent to the screen of my laptop words from his heart.

And so I have been given a diagnosis—leukemia, a curse or a gift? I have prayed and pondered how gracious my God has been in allowing me to see my mortality, to review my life, to draw closer to him, and to praise him.

These are the times God tries the heart, reveals his face, and draws us to places, well, I have never been before. . . . I have become utterly dependent upon the prayers of the saints, and God has performed miraculous acts even in my little isolation room. He alone deserves our praise.

He has shown me the joys of my wife's eyes, my children's voices, and the fulfillment of just dwelling upon the blessing they are to me. Wow! What have I been missing?

Jeff passed away not long after he e-mailed me. The funeral was held in a large church building, but it still couldn't hold the crowd.

I look forward to long conversations with Jeff on the other side of death, when we both can celebrate in the presence of the one who redeems all pain, answers all questions, and brings clear sight to all eyes.

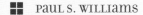 PAUL S. WILLIAMS

Who has God used to heal you physically, emotionally, or spiritually? How did God's love and his healing touch shine through those people in your time of need?

What is your experience of God's faithfulness in your life through a time of pain? Your story can help others in their time of need. Write about your experience and ask God to give you the opportunity to share your story with someone who needs to hear it.

Do everything without complaining or arguing, so that you may become blameless and pure, children of God without fault in a crooked and depraved generation, in which you shine like stars in the universe.

PHILIPPIANS 2:14-16

They Never Complain

Sarah has lived a lifetime in her tender 26 years. Her kidneys failed years ago, and she knows all too well the wearing nature of dialysis. For years she had been on the list for a transplant for both a kidney and pancreas. She just recently had the double transplant, and though the surgery was successful, there have been complications. But through it all, I've not heard Sarah complain—ever. In dealing with dialysis, waiting for a transplant, and now the nauseating side effects of that transplant, Sarah just doesn't complain.

Sarah is a great singer but doesn't get to sing much because she doesn't have the strength. Sarah is witty and intelligent, but a lot of people don't know because she doesn't get out much. Sarah can be the best kind of friend because she can speak from the rich depths of experience. Sadly, only a few know that friendship because of her limited time away from home and hospital.

But Sarah never complains. As a matter of fact, she smiles so big you can see it through the hospital mask she wears so often.

And then there is me—healthy, active, and blessed with many friends. And yet I complain. I think I need to spend a bit more time with Sarah—I have much to learn.

Chris used to be a great golfer, and still would be if not for his shoulders. While serving in the Army, Chris flew Apache helicopters and then trained other pilots on the Apache. It seems that the wear and tear on his rotator cuffs during active duty caused damage. He has already had several surgeries trying to repair his shoulders, with no positive results. Chris lives with constant chronic pain. But you'd never know it because he never complains.

Chris is a leader and a friend to many. As a result he is often in the middle of the crowd. That crowd will often pat him on the shoulder, resulting in shooting pain. But you will not find him complaining, not even wincing. He doesn't want to be the center of attention, nor does he want to embarrass others with his pain. So he just endures it.

And then there is me. I get a headache and want everyone to know. I had a little bout with tendonitis in my shoulder and whined for months. Maybe a little more time with Chris is just what the doctor ordered.

Chris and Sarah have been used by God to encourage me to complain less and be grateful more. I have much to learn, but I know just the friends to teach me.

 GREG ALLEN

What causes you to complain the most?
Why do you complain? What do you hope to
achieve through it?

Who do you know that has every right to complain
but doesn't? What specific lessons can you learn from
him or her today?

Jesus said, "In my Father's house are many rooms; if it were not so, I would have told you. I am going there to prepare a place for you. And if I go and prepare a place for you, I will come back and take you to be with me."

Lon Miller

The service ended with the fire bell signaling the last call. The chief handed Lon's 8-year-old son, Zach, his dad's helmet, and then Zach and his family walked through the column of saluting firefighters.

Zach marched forward with that helmet, held high. This little guy was so proud to be carrying his dad's helmet—he was so proud of his father. There wasn't a dry eye in the place.

The first time I met Lon was while he was touring our office building. He was our local fire inspector. Lon was a big guy, a firefighter, a former Navy man, and a local football hero. He also had a warm and inviting personality. Through the influence of some people on our staff, Lon and his family made a commitment to Christ. Lon was happy and life was good.

It was a tough day when he told me he was sure that he had Lou Gehrig's disease. Unfortunately, he had an aggressive version. In September Lon was running 10 miles a day and tossing his kids in the air. In February we were gathering to say good-bye to our 32-year-old friend.

Lon and I had been meeting together every week to talk about life and death, hope and grace. Through this whole time, Lon never lost his laughter, never lost the sparkle in his eye, and never quit living.

Lon wrote letters while he could—letters to his kids, his wife, and his friends. He wrote one that he asked me to read at his funeral service, and he gave me permission to share it here as well.

Well here we are, I'm finally home. Today most of you are still struggling with the fact that I'm really gone. It is OK to cry. I know that over the past few months I've cried a lot. Sarah knows, she and I have cried many nights together. However, as I look at the past year and how sad it has been, I can't help but think of the 31 years of laughter that I've been blessed with.

When my father died, all I could remember was this frail old man who had succumbed to a terrible disease. It wasn't until years later that I began to remember him as a very funny, very powerful man, and that's the person I choose to remember. I hope that from this day forward you remember me not as a man struggling for each breath or unable to use his legs anymore, but you remember me as a person who loved his kids, saw a hero in his wife, and had more friends than should have been allowed.

God put each and every one of us on this earth to live a life according to his teachings so that we might build a relationship with him. I know I have a relationship with God. It may not be a perfect one but then again, who is perfect? There is the fact that God gave us time on earth, how much time is up to him. How you choose to use this time is up to you.

I love you all. I bet I miss you all more than you could ever miss me. Well, here we are, I guess it's time to go home. Thanks. It's been fun!

Love forever and ever, Lon

 RICK RUSAW

How will people remember you when you are gone?
How do you want them to remember you?
What can you begin doing today that will lead people
to remember you the way you hope they will?

How you choose to use the time given to you is up to you.
How will you use the time that has been given to you by
your heavenly Father?

As Jesus was on his way, the crowds almost crushed him. And a woman was there who had been subject to bleeding for twelve years, but no one could heal her. She came up behind him and touched the edge of his cloak, and immediately her bleeding stopped. "Who touched me?" Jesus asked.

LUKE 8:42-45

Acquainted with the Principle

They almost crushed him. Jesus was on his way to visit the sick daughter of an influential man. As he walked, a great mob of people surrounded him, pressing in from all sides like cameramen at a celebrity arraignment. Suddenly, Jesus stopped. "'Who touched me?' Jesus asked. . . . Peter said, 'Master, the people are crowding and pressing against you'" (Luke 8:45).

I too am surrounded by a great mob—a crushing volume of electronic and print media competing for my attention. "A teenage boy was killed tonight in a drive-by shooting," the newscaster announces. "More at 11:00." But what if I don't want "more at 11:00"? What if my senses are on overload? Do I really need to see another death in an urban neighborhood? Don't I have better things to do with my time?

"One would think that several minutes of murder and mayhem would suffice as material for a month of sleepless nights," wrote Neil Postman in his book, *Amusing Ourselves to Death*. He was not a fan of the content of the 11:00 news. Henry David Thoreau would not have been either. He said, "If we read of one man robbed or murdered, we never need read of another. One is enough. If you are acquainted with the principle, why do you need a myriad of applications?"

Now there's a thought. If we're acquainted with the principle, do we really need example after example to burn the reality of tragedy and sadness into our minds?

There were a lot of needy people surrounding Jesus—a lot of stories worthy of the evening news. But Jesus never avoided suffering. In the midst of a very busy day, Jesus took time for one more sad story. "Who touched me?" he said. No matter how much suffering he had seen, Jesus still refused to turn away from suffering. He was still willing to be touched.

The woman had spent 12 years and all her money trying to get medical help. But the bleeding wouldn't stop. The hemorrhaging meant she was not only severely ill but also, according to religious law, unclean and therefore untouchable. Her last hope was the young rabbi.

She wouldn't dare approach him face-to-face. But perhaps in the large crowd, she could touch the hem of his robe without being noticed. But Jesus *did* notice her. He always notices. And she was healed.

We see so much bad news in the newspaper, on the Internet, and on television that we become desensitized. But Jesus invites us to a different perspective. Every drive-by shooting, suicide bombing, and armed robbery reminds us of the great suffering in the world. No matter how often we see the pain, we need to remember that these are real people with real needs. And Jesus wants me to touch those lives and meet those needs through his love. And maybe, if I remember the human story behind every headline, I too can find the strength to say one more time with Jesus, "Who touched me?"

■ ERIC SNYDER AND PAUL S. WILLIAMS

Do you find yourself feeling overwhelmed and depressed with all the suffering in your world, city, or even your own family? Take some time to write about the suffering or sadness you are experiencing, and then ask Jesus to come and bring healing.

How can you be the healing hands of Jesus today in the midst of the suffering of this world? What are some specific things you can do to reach out to others with the love of Jesus?

You are the body of Christ, and each one of you is a part of it.

1 corinthians 12:27

A Portrait of Christ

What did Jesus look like? The Scriptures don't tell us much about his physical appearance. He was Jewish and the son of a carpenter. Most Jewish men of that time were probably around 5' 6" tall. Was Jesus 5' 6"? Or was he my height of 6' 3", like I imagine him? The truth is, we don't know.

The Old Testament prophet Isaiah wrote that there was nothing desirable about the Messiah's appearance. That's all he said. Jesus was ordinary looking. I take some comfort in that, since I consider myself to be fairly ordinary looking too.

Most authors introduce their characters with very vivid descriptions, but it's rare for the Bible to offer a physical description of anyone, let alone Jesus. The many complex, well-rounded characters in the Bible are revealed to us through their words and actions, not their physical appearance.

And yet, over the centuries there has been a wide range of portraits of the Son of God. The question is, are any of them accurate?

Jesus looks different in every work of art that attempts to depict him, and how he is portrayed has changed through the centuries. According to Richard Wightman Fox, in the nineteenth century Americans from the working class made

Jesus "a democrat, a man of the people, a crucified carpenter."

Fox reminds us of H. Richard Niebuhr's admonition, "Jesus outdistances all efforts to contain him: think twice, therefore, before you dismiss someone else's view of him."

So what does Jesus look like?

Jesus is a black man named Martin, who came to the Mountaintop in Memphis in 1968. He is a small Macedonian woman named Teresa, who took on the burden of the poor in Calcutta. He is a white man named Billy, a southern preacher and friend of presidents.

He is the person seated next to you in the movie theater, and the person across town where you could never imagine yourself going for dinner. He

is the child with Down's Syndrome who hugs everyone she meets. He is the young mother out for a
stroll with her children.

The accurate picture of Jesus is the ever-present,
living body of Christ—his followers. Like it or not,
he is revealed to the world through the words and
actions of those who follow him. Alone, they may
not look like much. But put them all together, and
on their better days, the face of Jesus appears.

ERIC SNYDER AND PAUL S. WILLIAMS

As a child did you have a favorite picture of Christ?
Why do you think you were drawn to that image
of Jesus?

Who are the people that show you the face of Jesus?
In what ways can you begin to be the face of Christ to
those around you today?

In your hearts set apart Christ as Lord. Always be prepared to give an answer to everyone who asks you to give the reason for the hope that you have. But do this with gentleness and respect, keeping a clear conscience.

1 PeTer 3:15, 16

House Divided

When was the last time you heard someone "win" a theological argument? I thought so—I can't remember either. And, unfortunately, I'd have to admit to being involved in a few. I didn't win any of them. Neither did the other parties involved. It seems everybody loses when we argue. Meanwhile, the essence of the faith we're defending melts away in the heat of our argument, and witnesses to the whole affair walk away shaking their heads. Who could blame them? That brings to mind the story of a spiritual argument that turned *really* ugly.

Jesus said, "Any kingdom divided against itself will be ruined, and a house divided against itself will fall" (Luke 11:17). This statement was brought into sharp focus for me when I read about Sean and Melissa Davidson of Statesboro, Georgia, a young couple in their 30s. They had just seen the motion picture *The Passion of the Christ*, and on the way home they began discussing whether God as a heavenly Father was symbolic or literal.

When they arrived home, what had by then become a heated argument escalated into violence prompting both of them to call the police on *each other*. Mrs. Davidson said, "It was the dumbest thing we've ever done." The chief sheriff's deputy, Gene McDaniel, said, "I think they missed the point." I wholeheartedly agree with both statements.

Here's the kicker: they were both wrong. God is not human; he is a spirit. And he isn't symbolic; he's very real. There's another theological argument gone bad.

On more than one occasion, Jesus issued scathing denunciations against the religious leaders of his day. They had argued and legislated their way to a stand-alone system of legalism and self-declared righteousness, yet they had missed the point of what the spirit of the law conveyed. In so doing they had polarized people instead of drawing them together.

Could the same be true of us? Could we be like the young couple who was arrested for harming one another after an argument about God? Could we be so intent on proving our intellectual prowess that we prove our spiritual insensitivity instead? And what of those we have been commissioned to influence? Does God's household of faith appear divided to them?

In the Bible Paul tells us, "Don't have anything to do with foolish and stupid arguments, because you know they produce quarrels. And the Lord's servant must not quarrel; instead, he must be kind to everyone, able to teach, not resentful. Those who oppose him he must gently instruct, in the hope that God will grant them repentance leading them to a knowledge of the truth" (2 Timothy 2:23-25).

Have you ever been involved in a theological debate that did more harm than good? What happened to your relationship with that person?

Have you ever had a discussion about theology that was profitable and encouraging? What made the difference between the discussion and the argument?

*Jesus answered, "Everyone who drinks this water will be thirsty
again, but whoever drinks the water I give him will never thirst.
Indeed, the water I give him will become in him a spring of water
welling up to eternal life."*

JOHN 4:13, 14

Cup of Water

She didn't expect the water to taste so good. Her
name was not given, but we'll call her Samantha.
She was from across the tracks, a lower-class citi-
zen, undesirable. Samantha was even an outcast
among outcasts. Samantha had been married to
five different men and was currently living with a
sixth. Though she had been in many relationships,
Samantha was alone. She was at a famous well to
fill her jar with water so she could cook and clean,

coming at a time of day when she could avoid the disapproving glares of others.

Jesus came to the same well. She was shocked that he would even be there, much less ask her for a drink. That may not mean much to you, but it did to Samantha. You see, Jesus didn't have a cup from which to drink. In order to take a drink, Jesus would have to drink from *her* cup. That still may not mean much to you, but it turned Samantha's world upside down. Her cup was filled with the emptiness of broken marriages, the guilt of horrible decisions, and the shame of being an outcast.

But it did not keep Jesus from sharing the pain of her past. This man, this seventh man in her life, was about to offer a relationship of hope. Seven is called the number of perfection. I don't know if Samantha knew that. But I'm sure she knew that this seventh man was different from the others.

Tyler was drinking bad water. He had made some bad decisions in the past and was suffering the consequences. He had deceived his employer and his closest friends and had lost his career in his prime. His life's cup was filled with guilt.

Grady was a friend who knew about the deception and the guilt that haunted Tyler. Grady had a decision to make—to avoid Tyler like everybody else or take the risk and offer to drink from Tyler's cup.

But Grady cared for people, all people, especially people whom he called friend—especially a friend who needed him. So he invited Tyler to the usual hangout for a cup of coffee. Grady didn't intend to solve any problems. He only offered to trade a cup of guilt for a cup of friendship. I'd like to say all is well that ends well, but the story hasn't ended yet. Tyler's cup of guilt is still hanging around, but so is Tyler's friend.

God offers not only to take that cup but also to drink from it until the guilt is gone. Actually, that is what he has already done on the cross. God says that if you are burdened and stressed, he will exchange it all for a clean refreshing drink of living water. And many times he asks us, his children, to be his partners in bringing this cup of water to others in need.

 GreG ALLen

Are you drinking God's living water or your own cup of shame and guilt? How could your life change if you allowed God to take that cup of guilt from you?

Is there an acquaintance in your life that you've been avoiding but who needs a cup of friendship from you? How will you follow Jesus' example and drink from their cups?

Accept one another . . . just as Christ accepted you, in order to bring praise to God.

Romans 15:7

Josh and Jessica

One of the most respected men in the small town of Waynesville was Josh. He chose his words carefully. He didn't say a lot, but when he spoke, people listened.

Josh was the kind of man you wanted to be with because he was in love with life, and he seemed to know so much about it. He was kind, wise, and joyful.

Waynesville was a small town, where everybody knew everybody. And people thought that they knew everything there was to know about Jessica. But Jessica longed for someone to care for her as a person and not just for what she looked like. But because she didn't know how to get people to care for her in the way she needed, she developed a reputation for being inappropriate with men. As a result, she was condemned by everyone—everyone except Josh.

They met at the ballpark one Saturday when most families were watching their children play Little League. Josh knew her reputation. She knew his. Know what he said?

"I'm glad I finally got to meet you. I'm Josh. You're Jessica, right?"

And while the next five innings of Little League

were played, they sat beside the third base line and talked. A woman's life was significantly changed that night because one kind and respected man cared enough to talk and listen.

Timmy wasn't the smartest child in class, but he was the sweetest by far. Timmy embodied the perfect recipe for ridicule—a learning disability, a speech problem, and outdated clothes. One Friday his pencil broke and he didn't have another one; he asked Sally if he could borrow one of hers. She curtly replied, "No, I don't want you touching my stuff."

Fortunately, Miss Vencil was watching what was happening. She called Timmy to her desk and offered him two new pencils. She also gave him a gentle hug around the shoulder. Sharing pencils can make a little boy's day, but willingness to accept a person can change his life.

The Bible tells of a woman who was caught in the middle of a sinful act. Her name is not given. The religious people were not interested in who she was, just what she had done wrong. Indeed, what she had done was wrong, even in the eyes of Jesus. But rather than shunning, condemning, or ignoring her, Jesus talked to her and paid attention to her. He told her that he wasn't interested in reviewing the past, but wanted to give her a vision of the future.

I'd like to be like that. I want to be more interested in the hearts of people than in their mistakes. I'd like to be humble enough to acknowledge my own imperfections in order to accept other imperfect people. I want to be grateful for being accepted by the one who gives me a future worth living.

 GreG ALLen

When have you been treated unfairly, picked on, or excluded? What emotions come up when you think about those situations?

What are the lessons we can learn from Jesus' acceptance of those who others considered outcasts? Who do you know that needs the encouragement of your acceptance and kindness?

The LORD is close to the brokenhearted
and saves those who are crushed in spirit.
A righteous man may have many troubles,
but the LORD delivers him from them all.

PSALM 34:18, 19

Parking Cones on a Saturday Night

We hear a lot about single mothers these days, but there are many single dads too!

Marty is one of them. Although unfortunate circumstances ended his marriage, he treasures his relationship with his children Jeffrey and Kara. I see Marty with Kara often. He is very tender toward his daughter. Kara is 13, and she has autism.

For quite a while, Marty went without a job. Though he was having a tough time paying bills, he was always there for his children. No one would have blamed Marty if he had given up on life. His was estranged from his wife, he had no job, and he faced the struggles of parenting a special needs child. That is quite a formula for despair. But Marty did not give up on life.

Most every Saturday afternoon you could find Marty and Kara in an old pickup truck, placing big orange cones around the parking lot of his church. Hot, humid, cold, wet—it didn't matter—father and daughter saw to it that the cones were in place so that people coming to worship would know where to go.

After those Saturday night church services, Kara always came and found me. "Hi, Mr. Greg," she would say, followed by a big hug and a great smile.

Her dad would sit and wait for Kara to complete her
sweet ritual.

Marty was pretty much alone between visits with
his children. But he faithfully followed God, even
in the midst of loneliness. He had made mistakes
as a husband and father, but he wasn't going to
focus on the past. He was going to commit himself
to his children and his God. And every Saturday,
those parking cones reminded him where his
priorities were. The cones were there as boundary
markers, helping people move in the right direction on their way to church. For Marty, putting out
the cones helped him remember the important
things in his life—family and God.

The presence of God is not reserved for the perfect
family. God is with all those who long to belong to
his heavenly family. The Bible promises that God
is close to the brokenhearted—that includes Marty,

a single dad. I believe Marty and Kara have a keen awareness of God's presence. Kara carries with her the uncanny sense of peace that only God can give, and Kara extends that peace to her father. Kara's smile is contagious. It has spread to her father, to me, and to most everyone who encounters this daddy-daughter duo. I can't exactly explain it. As a matter of fact, I don't even want to try. I just want to *enjoy it*.

 GREG ALLEN

When have you experienced a "keen awareness of God's presence"? When have you longed for that presence but not felt it?

What things can you do to remind others of God's presence? How can you shine the light of Jesus into someone's life today?

Taking the child in his arms, Jesus said to [his disciples],
"Anyone who welcomes a little child like this on my behalf
welcomes me, and anyone who welcomes me welcomes my
Father who sent me."

Mark 9:36, 37, *NLT*

Not Easy to Come By

Ruddy Hines had a big problem.

He was a student at Martin Luther King Elementary
School in Washington, D.C., and one day he got
mad and called his best friend Raymond a bad
name. This of course had a terrible effect on their
relationship. Even though Ruddy said he was sorry,
things just weren't the same. Ruddy didn't know
what to do about it, so he wrote a letter to another

friend, Ron, with whom he corresponded regularly, to ask for advice. Though his friend was a busy man, he could always count on him in difficult times.

Ron always answered Ruddy's letters even though he was a busy man. Actually, he was one of the busiest men in the world because "Ron" was Ronald Reagan, president of the United States.

President Reagan wrote back to his regular correspondent Ruddy and said, "I'm sorry to hear about your problem with your friend Raymond. You did right in telling him you were sorry. Maybe you need to do a little more. . . . Go to him when you can talk quietly without others around. Tell him good friends aren't easy to come by. Tell him you were upset and not thinking straight when you called him what you did, but you didn't mean it, and you want him for your best friend."

The leader of the free world had given Ruddy's dilemma the consideration that was due entire nations. Some would call this an extravagance. Jesus called it living for the kingdom of God.

Befriending others just because they can help us get ahead makes us small. Conversely, a sign of true greatness is devoting attention to someone from whom there can be no perceived gain. What did Ronald Reagan gain from corresponding with an elementary school student in Washington, D.C.? If nothing else, he gained my respect for following the example of an even greater world leader.

Jesus sat down and called his 12 ambitious followers to himself. He had a little child stand in front of them. Then he wrapped his arms around the child and said, "Whoever welcomes one of these little children in my name welcomes me; and . . . the one who sent me" (Mark 9:37).

Ruddy Hines wrote President Reagan back to tell him his advice worked, "Raymond and I are friends again, like before." There is rarely a convenient time to address the relational struggles of anyone, let alone an elementary school child. But greatness understands that good friends aren't easy to come by and is less concerned with convenience than with ending cold wars . . . both large and small, wherever they may be.

■ ERIC SNYDER FOR RICK RUSAW

Who had the greatest positive impact on you as a child?
What did he or she do that made such a difference in
your life?

How can you reach out to the children in your life?
What is something you could do to impact them
for eternity?

Encourage those who are timid. Take tender care of those who are weak. Be patient with everyone. See that no one pays back evil for evil, but always try to do good to each other and to everyone else.

1 THESSALONIANS 5:14, 15, *NLT*

A Colorado Grandmother

On a recent trip, I was hiking up from Twin Owls trailhead to Gem Lake. The August monsoon moisture had been evident all week, guaranteeing thunderstorms virtually every afternoon. I wanted to get up and back down the mountain before the sky clouded over. I came upon an older woman, grandmotherly in appearance. She carried a walking stick that appeared to have been picked up early on the trail, and she took very slow and deliberate steps forward. I was surprised she had successfully hiked that far up the 8,900-foot mountain. From her pace I assumed she must have been on the trail a full hour before me, maybe longer.

As I prepared to pass, I gently informed her a hiker was coming up behind her, to her left, so as not to startle her. She greeted me cheerily and asked if I knew how much farther it was to the top. I assured her it was only another tenth of a mile or so, and I quickly moved by on my journey.

I hiked right past Gem Lake and down the back side of Lumpy Ridge about six-tenths of a mile or so, to a place where there is an unusual rock formation that puts me in mind of an angel statue. I took off my backpack, drank some iced tea, and looked at the northwestern sky. In the distance just beyond the northern boundary of the park, I could see clouds beginning to build. I turned and headed

back up to Gem Lake and then back down the
mountain toward the Twin Owls trailhead.

As I rounded a corner, I saw the woman again. I
asked how she was enjoying her hike. She told me
it had been a long time since she had hiked in the
Rockies. She said, "I parked my car at the Gem
Lake trailhead. I guess there was a closer place to
park?" I let her know there was, indeed, a closer
place to park, and I suggested she should be careful
to take a left turn at the trail junction to get to her
trailhead parking lot. She assured me she would.

I quickly descended to Twin Owls trailhead and
drove the mile or so over to the Gem Lake trailhead. Then I grabbed my backpack and trekking
poles and headed up the trail. A few "early-warn-
ing" raindrops started to fall as I hiked up the trail
at a rapid pace. As I came around a bend about a
half-mile from the trailhead, there she was.

"Oh, it's you again," she said. "I thought you said you parked at the other trailhead."

"I did," I replied. "I drove over to this trailhead just to see how your hike was coming along."

"Well, that was very thoughtful of you. I truly appreciate it. I truly do."

We talked for several minutes and as she got in her car to leave, she said, "I'll remember you. Yes, sir, I will."

Of all the miles I've hiked, the most memorable miles are not about the scenery. They are about the people I've encountered on the journey. The most beautiful parts of God's creation are the people. We are, after all, the only part of creation made in the image of God himself.

 PAUL S. WILLIAMS

Have you met anyone along your life's journey who
has left a lasting impression? Who was it?
What was it about your encounter that you will
never forget?

When have you gone the extra mile to show care and
concern for a "fellow traveler"? Describe this time.
In what ways can you touch someone else as you
journey today?

It is written, "How beautiful are the feet of those who bring good news!" . . . Consequently, faith comes from hearing the message, and the message is heard through the word of Christ.

ROMANS 10:15, 17

It Just Begins to Live That Day

A word is dead when it is said, some say.
I say it just begins to live that day.

These words of Emily Dickinson express my thoughts regarding talking with others about faith. I am not a natural evangelist. Never have been. No seatmate on a plane need worry about a Bible-thumping lecture from me. When I was younger and tried to evangelize, the words stumbled and crashed off my tongue. The pressure to convince a person to change the course of his or her life during a 20-minute conversation left me sweaty and nauseous. But I have finally come to understand what God asks of me when it comes to speaking with others about my Christian faith.

I used to have a lot of answers to questions no one was asking. When I spoke about faith, my neighbors responded by cocking their heads to one side. My dog does that when she's confused. I think I confused a lot of neighbors.

It reminds me of the first part of that Emily Dickinson poem: "A word is dead when it is said, some say."

Now that I'm older, I have grown much more comfortable with conversations about faith. I understand evangelism is an accumulation of honest discussions. The questions of unbelief are many, and the people in my neck of the woods are not hesitant in pointing them out. And I understand their doubts. The same questions puzzle me too. I often discover that admitting what I do not understand is what moves the conversation along. That and taking the time to really listen. Truly attending to what another has to teach me and valuing the relationship for its own sake is what it means to share your faith.

I have a friend who once said, "Thanks for being there to shine the light a step or two in front of me on the journey." I took his word as highest praise. For the life of me, I don't know how he could have seen anything with the battery-depleted penlight I was carrying. I did not speak persuasively. But the smallest of words shed just enough light for the two of us, and we both are on the journey still.

That reminds me of the second half of that
Emily Dickinson poem: "I say it just begins to
live that day."

Christianity thrives from ear to ear overheard.
Through the din of our own tired, conflicted lives,
the Word lives on. And that is a miracle.

A word is dead when it is said, some say.
I say it just begins to live that day.

PAUL S. WILLIAMS

How do you feel about sharing your faith with others?
Why do you think you feel this way?

How could you initiate a conversation about faith in a
natural way? What are common interests and topics
that you could use to talk about how God has worked in
your life?

If we confess our sins, [God] is faithful and just and will forgive us our sins and purify us from all unrighteousness.

Imperfect

I was in the main US Airways Club in Philadelphia at mid-morning. With the early bank of flights already departed and the noon bank yet to arrive, there were relatively few of us eating our complimentary banana nut muffins.

But there wasn't the marvelous silence you might expect there to be in a nearly empty lounge. About 30 feet away, standing in the middle of the club, speaking into his cell phone, was a loud talker. From my observations, the vast majority of loud talkers are male. Along with their ability to speak loudly enough for crowds of 20,000 to hear, they are also blessed with the ability to speak almost incessantly about nothing.

"Yeah, Jim. I'm telling you, how can we possibly win that market without a sales rep stationed there? I mean, you know, Jim, you've got to have a sales rep close by to conquer a marketplace. Without a sales rep permanently in the area, you just won't do well."

I believe Jim understood. There was no doubt that everyone in the airport lounge understood.

I was flying to Tampa in late November when the sounds emanating from the lady behind me reminded me that I hadn't gotten a flu shot yet. She coughed without ceasing, and over the course of the two-and-a-half-hour flight, she failed to cover her mouth even once.

And so it goes.

I began to wonder, *What do I do that drives people to distraction?*

I've been told that I can walk through a foyer full of people at church and never once speak to a single soul. I am also given to moods of considerable darkness. As much as I try, I will never conquer all of my bad habits.

I will grow through the grace of God, but I will never be perfect. And neither will anyone else. There is a touch of sadness for me because of this fact, and there is also an awareness that this should make me more gracious toward the flaws of others.

So the next time I encounter Mr. Loud-Talker or Ms. Coughing Fit, I'm going to ask God to remind me that nobody's perfect—but that everyone is an object of his love.

PAUL S. WILLIAMS

What are some of your pet peeves? List a few.
What causes you to feel so annoyed by these things?

How can remembering God's love for each of us change
your outlook on the little things that annoy you?
How can you show grace to a "loud talker" in your life?

By this all men will know that you are my disciples, if you love one another.

JOHN 13:35

Cream-Filled Donuts

When I was a child, I loved my Saturday morning routine. It was my favorite part of the weekend. All through the school week, I couldn't wait for Saturday morning to come—two cream-filled donuts and a blessed 48 hours before my return to the classroom.

I woke up one winter Saturday morning, and, as usual, headed off to Hoffman's Bakery. But something happened that day that forever changed how I viewed my Saturday morning ritual. No terrible tragedy. No screeching tires or wailing sirens. Just a simple baker's mistake.

But on that fateful day, the regular baker wasn't there. A new face was making the donuts, but that seemed to be no cause for concern. The counter lady was the same, and she didn't seem to be paying much mind to the substitute baker.

I ordered my usual. The lady put them in the bag and I headed home. Then I bit into my cream-filled donut.

The baker had injected poison into the donut! That's right, poison. I spit the donut out after the first bite and ran upstairs. I woke up Dad and told him there was poison in the donuts. Dad said, "Oh," and fell back asleep. I went to Mom's side of the bed and told her there was poison in the donuts. She stumbled out of bed in her flannel nightgown and came downstairs to investigate. Thank God for mothers! As she came into the family room, I showed her the evidence. "See," I said. "It even looks like poison. It's kinda yellow." Mom took a sniff and authoritatively announced there was no reason to panic. No poison was being dispensed at Hoffman's Bakery. She said in a manner designed to assure no additional questioning, "It's Bavarian cream, that's all. It's a different kind of cream."

Bavarian cream! No one had asked my opinion or sought my advice about any Bavarian cream. No one called me the night before to let me know there would be a change in the menu. The substitute baker just hid the vile stuff inside the innocent donut and sold it to unsuspecting folks all over Akron, Ohio.

Mom went back to bed. The donuts were inedible, and nothing could be done. I got out a bowl of cereal and sulked through the rest of Saturday morning cartoons.

I don't eat donuts much anymore. But I still remember the day the substitute baker taught me that what something looks like on the outside doesn't necessarily guarantee what's beneath the surface.

Maybe that's what the Bible means when it says "By their fruit you will recognize them" (Matthew 7:16). So I pray that people will know me by the sweetness of Christ in my life and that there will be no trace of the poison of sin.

PAUL S. WILLIAMS

When have you judged something by what's on the
surface and then discovered that you were wrong?
What people have you judged by what was on the
outside instead of what was on the inside?

Does your life show the truth of who you are?
What changes need to be made in your life so that
people will see the sweetness of Christ in you?

Whoever wants to save his life will lose it, but whoever loses his life for me will find it. What good will it be for a man if he gains the whole world, yet forfeits his soul? Or what can a man give in exchange for his soul?

MATTHEW 16:25, 26

Benning Wentworth

Take the Rockefellers, Roosevelts, and Kennedys; wrap them into one family dynasty, and you will come close to the power and fame of the Wentworths of eighteenth-century New Hampshire. They wore the finest clothes, controlled a vast expanse of land, and wielded enormous influence for generations. One Wentworth is remembered for having built a fascinating house on the banks of Little Harbor in Portsmouth,

New Hampshire. The famous hotel Wentworth by the Sea is named after him.

Another Wentworth, Benning Wentworth, was governor of New Hampshire from 1741 to 1767. He was powerful and wealthy. In addition to coming from an aristocratic family, he made his own fortune in timber and land speculation. When the General Assembly refused to purchase a large house for him in downtown Portsmouth, he built his own unusual home in 1753. It became the social and political center for the region.

Benning Wentworth outlived his wife and all three of his sons. He remarried a younger woman from a respectable family and died in 1770. And that's about it. With the exception of other legislative details and business transactions, these few facts are all we know about one of the most influential men ever to have lived in New Hampshire.

The Wentworths prompted me to think: *What kind of legacy will I leave behind? How will I be remembered? Will I be remembered at all? How do I want to be remembered?*

This is the story of another influential man—in fact, he is the most influential person in history. And yet, he never built any buildings. As far as we know, he never owned a home. He was dirt-poor. He did not hold public office and never sought political power. He never married and, consequently, had no descendants. His parents were rural folk—his father, a carpenter. But I daresay that everyone has heard this man's name—he is Jesus.

One of the wealthiest men in all of colonial America, a man who distinguished himself in serving the longest term ever as a royal governor in New Hampshire, a man who exercised more political power than 10 of his contemporaries put

together—this man is scarcely remembered at all.
Why the difference between these two?

Benning Wentworth invested shrewdly to amass a
huge fortune. Jesus invested himself in the spiritual welfare of people. Wentworth exercised political
power for the king of England. Jesus emptied himself to honor the God of the universe. The printed
profile of Wentworth's life is facts and figures.
The written record of Jesus is about relationships.
Wentworth built an earthly estate. Jesus established
a heavenly kingdom.

I suppose we can conclude that whether we are
remembered or forgotten will be determined
largely by whether we are willing to serve or insist
on being served.

What will be your legacy?

How do you want to be remembered when you are gone? What do you hope people will say about you?

In the movie *Dead Poets Society*, a professor whispered to his students, "Carpe diem. Seize the day." Has God been whispering these same words in your ear? How will you *seize the day* today and leave a legacy that endures?

May the God of hope fill you with all joy and peace as you trust in him, so that you may overflow with hope by the power of the Holy Spirit.

ROMANS 15:13

Joy in the Balance

Our attitude colors our view on everything. So I can think of few higher priorities than developing a positive attitude about life itself.

The Bible encourages us to adopt a healthy perspective of all things. It reads, "Be joyful always; pray continually; give thanks in all circumstances, for this is God's will for you" (1 Thessalonians 5:16-18).

We've all known someone who seems to thrive on being negative and sour. In light of God's call to joy, there's no case to be made for that outlook. But to overreact and go to the opposite extreme is just as perplexing. Some believers would interpret that verse to mean that we're duty-bound to be happy, bubbly, and ecstatic every single moment. I find people like this more than a bit challenging.

The forced happiness of some Christians is shallow and plastic. They equate joy with outward cheer and insist God wants us to be animated and bouncy. It seems that they cannot allow themselves, or others, the freedom to contemplate some of the serious issues we face.

An elderly gentleman checked into a nursing home and was immediately greeted by four women residents.

One of the ladies asked him, "You're new here, aren't you?"

"Yes," he said.

Then another of the women asked him where he had come from. He replied, "I just finished a 20-year prison term."

"Why were you there so long?" one of the others wanted to know.

"I was in prison because I murdered my wife."

Immediately the fourth lady chimed in, "Oh, then that means you're single!"

We might call that an unhealthy optimism!

No, thinking we have joy just because we act happy

outwardly simply won't do. Forgive me, but life just isn't that simple.

The Bible tells us our attitude is to be one in which we can be joyful always, pray continually, and give thanks in all circumstances. I see that as maintaining the delicate balance between idealism and realism. It recognizes joy as a *mindset*, not an animated countenance. Joy is an attitude that exists only when we strive to live in a constant awareness of God's companionship. True joy gladly acknowledges that we have no control over the circumstances we encounter, but virtually complete control over how we react to them, whatever they are. That is joy in the balance.

Is there someone in your life who always seems to see the glass half full? In contrast, do you know someone who always insists the glass is half empty?
Who would you rather be with? Why?

True joy is an attitude that exists in a constant awareness of God's companionship. When troubles arise does your life still show others true joy in the Lord?
How can you cultivate "joy in the balance" in your own life so that seekers will see Jesus' joy in you?

Let your light shine before men, that they may see your good deeds and praise your Father in heaven.

MATTHEW 5:16

Talk or Walk?

At the 1992 Democratic Convention, Bill Clinton told the American people that his faith in God would play a major role in his leadership.

Press coverage was devoted to his church attendance and prayer life. "My faith in God is a source of pride to me," he said. "The fact that I have a deep faith in God and a sense of trying to do the right thing should be reassuring to the people."

Many people have discovered, just as President Clinton did, how dangerous it is to speak publicly about one's faith and then later have to air your dirty linen in public. It is far better to *live* faith quietly than to *speak* of faith loudly, only to be labeled a hypocrite when you fail.

A magazine article some years ago carried the story of a woman who observed a young man board a bus she was riding from Flagstaff, Arizona, to Albuquerque, New Mexico. He made his way down the aisle and sat in the seat behind her. The night was cold and the bus warm; and in just a few minutes, he fell fast asleep.

After some time he woke up and asked the driver what time they would arrive at his destination. "We passed there some time ago," the driver replied. The boy's shoulders drooped as he walked back to his seat. Distressed and bewildered he walked back to the driver and asked if he could get off the bus and walk back to the missed station. The driver insisted it was too far and too cold. He would have to ride to Albuquerque.

The woman who observed all this was ultimately on her way back home to Wisconsin after serving as a volunteer teacher in a Native American mission school. As they approached Albuquerque, she knew the boy had to be terrified. How would he navigate the big, frightening city?

"Are you afraid?" she asked him.

"Yes," he admitted. "My sister and mother were waiting for me back there."

The woman encouraged him to sit with her. She told the driver she would make sure the boy got on the right bus when they arrived in Albuquerque.

And she convinced the driver to put him on the right bus without paying any additional fare.

The young man was deeply grateful. They had ridden on for about 10 minutes when her new young friend leaned toward her and in a reverent voice asked, "Are you a Christian?"

Jesus once told a story about two people and the responsibilities they had been assigned. One said he would get the job done, but he didn't. The other said he wouldn't do his job, but then went on to complete it in fine order.

Guess which one Jesus commended? Jesus was more pleased with the results of a quiet walk than he was with the noise of empty talk. The life you *actually live* makes more of an impact on others than anything they might hear you say.

What does your life say to those around you?
How do your actions show that you are a follower
of Christ?

Have you experienced any "divine appointments"—
times when God brought someone into your path so
that you might show him his love? If so, reflect on that
experience in writing. If not, write a prayer, asking God
to open your eyes to these opportunities.

For to me, to live is Christ and to die is gain.

PHILIPPIANS 1:21

Priorities

When we were young, it seemed pretty simple to figure out our priorities—do well in school, go to church, and don't get into trouble. Easy enough, right? As we get older though, it becomes more complicated.

My grandmother somehow managed to keep her priorities fairly simple. I remember her as one of those grandmothers who was always old, even when she was relatively young. She moved at a slow pace. She always wore a wig—and not because she needed to. In fact, she had beautiful long hair, with very little gray. But she said it was too tiresome to "put it up," so she simply plopped on a wig every day. She regularly convinced family members to join her in music sessions with the guitar, ukulele, or accordion, because "no one knew how to make good music" on the radio anymore.

We all had our fair share of laughs about Grandma's unusual habits and her amusing sayings. But there's one thing she taught me that I never joked about and that I've never forgotten. From the time I was a very young girl, Grandma made sure I had my priorities in order. She said that life goes by way too fast, and before you know it, you're an old woman. So make your life count for God, Grandma said. According to Grandma, it didn't matter how many pairs of shoes you owned or what your house looked like. The only thing that mattered was how many people had heard about Jesus because of you.

Something that always bothered me about Grandma was how often she talked about death. One day I told her how morbid I found the topic. She simply shrugged her shoulders and pointed to a plaque on the living room wall.

Years ago, Grandma had crafted this piece of art from a church bulletin. She carefully cut out the poem and surrounding flowers printed on yellow paper, mounted it on a piece of wood, shellacked it, and hung it up right by her front door so that every time you opened the door, you were forced to read it.

That plaque summarized my grandma's biggest priority—telling others about her Savior, Jesus. I have her old Bible that survived five floods. But that old piece of homemade art was the only thing I wanted once my grandma did pass away. All the other antiques and jewelry were passed out among family members. But oddly enough, no one was ever able to find her handmade plaque. I figure someone threw it out and won't admit it.

I'm OK with its loss though, because the words on Grandma's plaque have now become a part of me—*my* priority. Its words are not always easy to put into practice, but I try because I believe those words with all my heart.

Only one life, 'twill soon be past.
Only what's done for Christ will last.

 LISA JONES

Who has shown you how to have your priorities in order?
What about his or her life inspires you?

How do you feel about the poem: "Only one life, 'twill
soon be past. Only what's done for Christ will last"?
What steps might you take to make this the main
priority of your life?

Jesus said, "Take my yoke upon you and learn from me, for I am gentle and humble in heart, and you will find rest for your souls. For my yoke is easy and my burden is light."

MATTHEW 11:29, 30

It's All About Speed

While on a trip I was using my $3.50 in-flight headphones to listen to the channel that features the pilots and air traffic controllers communicating. "Can I get that up to mach .81?" the pilot of our flight asked the controller at the FAA's Denver center.

"Your company is always in such a hurry," the controller grumbled, as he granted the captain's request. I wasn't complaining. Time is money. A few minutes saved in the air meant I could get to my meeting on the ground that much sooner.

When I'm leaving town, I leave instructions for my staff via cell phone while I drive to the airport. While I'm waiting at the gate, I pore over the mail I've collected from the office. At 10,000 feet I open my laptop and write. I want to make every minute count. It's all about top efficiency—speed.

I've found that speed gets noticed. It is praised by others, especially those who speak of "return on investment" or "increased efficiencies." But when we go speeding through life, it's not long before we no longer appreciate those who travel at anything less than breakneck speed.

There is a slogan taught to young drivers: Speed kills. The same slogan could be taught to the speed-obsessed in every other facet of life. Speed kills creativity. Speed kills deep relationships. Speed kills our opportunities to rest and abide. Speed kills our ability to walk with others through the valley of the shadow of death. All it really helps us do is avoid true intimacy.

Small-town folks seldom major in speed. They focus instead on the long haul and major in building relationships. They remember the ending to the old fable about the tortoise and the hare.

Once I was in a country church near the Ohio-Pennsylvania border. The church had been there for 150 years. It was a medium-sized church. About 200 people gathered there every Sunday. The people in the church were busy, just like everyone is, but they didn't seem to be in much of a *hurry*. They had discovered that the truly important seldom has much to do with the seemingly urgent. I know Jesus gave us work to do, but did he really expect us to do it at breakneck speed?

I notice that the more the church looks like a corporation, the more speed matters. The more the church looks like the person of Jesus, the more willingness there is to slow down and remember that his yoke is easy, and his burden is light.

PAUL S. WILLIAMS

In what ways is your life all about speed?
What is speed killing in your life?

What are the most truly important issues in your life?
What seemingly urgent things could you cut out of your life so that you can pursue the truly important?

Peter got down out of the boat, walked on the water and came toward Jesus. But when he saw the wind, he was afraid and, beginning to sink, cried out, "Lord, save me!"

MATTHEW 14:29, 30

A Sinking Feeling

The disciples of Jesus had been rowing all night against the wind and waves of the Sea of Galilee. Very early in the morning, Jesus appeared to them, walking on the water. Most of the disciples thought they were seeing a ghost. Jesus said, "It is I." Then Peter said, "Lord, it's you." Then he boldly called out to Jesus, "Can I come walk with you?" Jesus said, "Come." Peter threw off his jacket and stepped over the edge of the boat.

What most people remember about the story is that Peter quickly took his eyes off Jesus and sank into the raging sea. The Son of God had to pick Peter up and drag him back, soaking wet, to the boat. We are not sure what caused Peter to lose his focus on Jesus. Maybe it wasn't just the wind and the waves that made him divert his eyes. Whatever the reason, Peter took his eyes off Jesus; and when he did, he failed.

We've heard the saying "nothing ventured, nothing gained." But have you ever risked and lost? Old impetuous Peter was always jumping out ahead of the rest of the disciples, usually getting into trouble as a result. Most of the time when he opened his mouth, it was to change feet. But it was also Peter who served God boldly and significantly because he was willing to put his faith, his abilities, and his life at risk. More so than the other disciples, Peter would stretch himself to try the impossible.

Let's suppose I didn't know whether I could walk. So I purchase motivational tapes on walking. I go to seminars on how to walk. I listen to inspirational music about walking. Yet I will never know if I am *able* to walk until I actually take a step and risk falling down.

Can you recall those moments when you wish you had taken a chance? Are there words you wish you had spoken, actions you wish you had taken? Stepping out of the boat isn't easy, especially if you've sunk in the past. But we need to be free to fail. It is only then that we are free to succeed. The great inventor Charles Kettering said, "You never stub your toe standing still."

What is often overlooked in Peter's sinking story is that Peter *walked on the water*. None of the other disciples even asked if they could come out. None of the other disciples jumped over the edge of the boat. It was Peter who put something at risk, and for a few moments, with his eyes fixed on Jesus, he experienced the miraculous. And it was Peter who later became a leader and founder of the church of that same Jesus. The steps he took in faith then reverberate to us even now. What will God do with you if you step out of the boat?

RICK RUSAW AND ERIC SNYDER

Are you a risk taker or do you find yourself staying
"in the boat" where life is more predictable?
How would your life be different today if you had
taken some of those risks that you chose to avoid?

In what ways do you need to fix your eyes on Jesus
and trust him to do the miraculous in your life?
Ask God to reveal ways you need to "step out of the
boat" in your life today.

Reckless words pierce like a sword,

but the tongue of the wise brings healing.

PROVERBS 12:18

Word Power

Did you ever use this old saying when you were
a kid: "Sticks and stones may break my bones,
but words will never hurt me"? While it may be
the standard line to use when you're being called
names on the playground, the fact is that words
do hurt.

Can you remember some of those verbal assaults
you received in grade school? "You're too tall, too

short, too skinny, too fat . . ." Maybe you're still trying to forget what was said.

Words are so small, yet they are so powerful. Most of us have been marked by carelessly spoken words. And sometimes it's the words that are *not* said that can hurt the most—words like: I love you, I need you, I forgive you, or I'm sorry.

Many of us struggle with an empty ache because of the words we long to hear.

I used to live in Cincinnati, Ohio. During the 1970s the University of Cincinnati built a large dormitory some 20 stories high. The construction took several years and a large sum of money. But when the building was finished, it was discovered that the foundation was unstable. As a result, no one ever was able to occupy the dormitory. On a Sunday morning in 1991, the building was imploded. It took only 11.1 seconds and a fraction of the construction cost to make the vacant dormitory collapse to the ground.

It is much easier to tear down than to build up.

People can be like that dormitory. Work and care over a lifetime are needed to build us up into stable, healthy people. But a few careless words can tear a person down in a matter of seconds. Sometimes words scar a person for life.

The apostle James marveled at how such a small thing—the tongue—can have tremendous power. He writes, "All kinds of animals, birds, reptiles and creatures of the sea . . . have been tamed by man, but no man can tame the tongue" (James 3:7, 8).

We need to choose our words carefully. Think about the words you've spoken today. Have they been good, positive, encouraging words? Or were they spoken in anger or frustration? The tongue has the power to create or destroy. May God help us to be powerful builders who create a foundation of wisdom, love, and assurance with our words.

RICK RUSAW

How have words impacted who you have become?
What words continue to echo in your heart—both
positively and negatively?

As Rick suggests, we need to learn to use our tongues
to build people up rather than tear them down. What
careless or harsh words have you spoken this past week?
What encouraging words can you speak today?

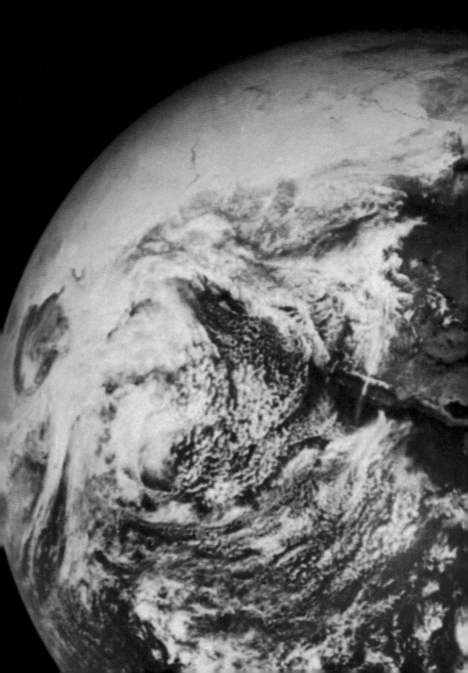

Jesus [said]: "'Love the Lord your God with all your heart and with all your soul and with all your mind.' This is the first and greatest commandment. And the second is like it: 'Love your neighbor as yourself.'"

MATTHEW 22:37-39

Perspective

Why do you do the things you do? What causes you to make the choices you make? When you decide something is right or wrong, how do you draw that conclusion? What shapes the way you see the world?

In his book *Divine Conspiracy*, Dallas Willard says, "Every last one of us has a 'kingdom'—a realm that is uniquely our own, where our choice determines what happens."

A recent poll concluded that the chief influences of American culture are movies, television, popular music, the Internet, and schools. They shape the way we think, feel, and react.

Each of us has a worldview. That worldview determines how we understand ourselves and the people around us. It determines how we navigate life.

Many take the view: "Eat, drink, and be merry, for tomorrow we die." Some call it life in the fast lane. Unfortunately, for many it becomes a short road to a quick end. It would take a long time to tally all the celebrities whose fast-lane life choices drove them to an early grave.

Others adopt the worldview: "Look out for Number One." They believe that the end justifies the means, and they'll do almost anything to get ahead. They usually don't start out that way. First it's just a little white lie that they believe won't really make much difference. And then one day that little white lie has turned into a felony that tears life apart.

Some wander from one worldview to another, never really deciding what they believe. They are thrown about by every wave on the sea, with no sails and a missing rudder.

What is your worldview? What shapes the decisions you make? What lenses give you perspective?

Jesus speaks about seeing life from a kingdom perspective—seeing life the way God sees it. His message is as countercultural today as it was in his own day. The message of Jesus invites us to see beyond ourselves. He challenges us to give up the worldview that leaves us rudderless and with no wind in our sails. He wants us to see our lives as he sees our lives—full of potential and possibility that will be realized only through relationships of love and service, a life whose potential will be achieved only if we worship God and live as Christ lived.

On his last day of public ministry, Jesus told those gathered with him how he wanted them to live. His instructions were incredibly simple—the simplest worldview in existence: "Love the Lord. . . . Love your neighbor" (Matthew 22:37, 39).

Let those two instructions shape your world, and you'll never regret a single day of your life.

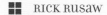 RICK RUSAW

Have you ever thought about your own worldview?
What shapes your perspective on life?

How does your worldview compare to the one Jesus
spoke of—to love the Lord and love others?
How can you live in that love?

When [Jesus] had finished washing [the disciples'] feet, he put on his clothes and returned to his place. . . . "I have set you an example that you should do as I have done for you. . . . Now that you know these things, you will be blessed if you do them."

JOHN 13:12, 15, 17

The Purpose of Power

There's a very simple rule you should follow when you travel. When you are in a security line at the airport, don't say anything! Unfortunately, I forgot that rule. I was late for my plane. Slow traffic, bad directions, and poor planning all contributed to my lateness. Still, if I could get to the gate, there was a chance I could make my flight.

And that's when I broke the rule.

The good news was that I was at a small airport, and I didn't have far to go to get to the gate. The bad news was that it was a small airport, and I don't think they'd had a passenger to screen during the past 18 months!

The guy looking at the screen must have thought I had Jimmy Hoffa in my bag. The screener was new, and overly thorough. I lost my head for a moment and said to no one in particular, "Must be Junior's first day." That comment received a knowing smile from an older lady in security, but a glare from Junior. Guess who didn't make his flight!

Trouble was, I knew better! Not only that, I understood Junior's thought process. I had been in his position for the first time when I was in the fifth grade. That's when I got the belt—that white belt that goes across your chest with the little badge that says Safety Patrol. I had arrived. I was among the chosen! I had a belt and a badge. I had *power*.

For my first assignment, I was stationed where the buses arrived in the school's circle drive. I was going to take care of every problem related to rowdy students and wayward cars. As the newest Safety Patrol officer, I was going to fix Elmcrest Elementary School.

Power is intoxicating. And as the old saying goes, "Absolute power corrupts absolutely." I think that's why Jesus had so much to say about power. He told us that those who really had power and knew how to use it correctly could be observed serving.

You see, serving others is the greatest expression of power. No one ever had more power than Jesus. And how did he use that power? He took a towel and a basin, and he washed his disciples' feet.

That's right. The eternal God, creator of the universe, washed dirty feet.

So the next time you find yourself in a position to make someone miss a flight or have the chance to belittle someone because you're important, remember: Life is not about a belt and a badge. Life is about a towel and a basin.

RICK RUSAW

Think back on your life—who are the people in power
that you have respected and learned the most from?
Now think back to those in power whom you have
disliked and do not respect. What is the difference
in the way the two types of people use their power?

Who are the people over whom you have power?
What are some ways you can begin to pick up the
towel and basin and serve them as Christ did?

May the words of my mouth and the meditation of my heart
be pleasing in your sight,
O LORD, my Rock and my Redeemer.

PSALM 19:14

The Last Freedom

The famous psychologist Dr. Viktor Frankl, a prison camp survivor, wrote, "We who lived in concentration camps can remember the men who walked through the huts comforting others, giving away their last piece of bread. They may have been few in number, but they offer sufficient proof that everything can be taken from a man but one thing: the last of the human freedoms—to choose one's attitude in any . . . circumstances, to choose one's own way."

In December 1995 at the age of 43, Jean-Dominique
Bauby suffered a massive stroke. At the time of
his death, he was the editor-in-chief of the
French *Elle* magazine. When I read of his death,
I was deeply touched, primarily because I had
previously read his fascinating book, *The Diving
Bell and the Butterfly*.

In the book Bauby recounted his tragic transforma-
tion from active father to prisoner, trapped
in a body that could not move. This successful
father of two young children had, without warning,
suddenly been placed in what he described
as a "cocoon-like" prison.

It is inspiring to learn what Bauby, despite his
immobility, managed to accomplish. His previous
life having ended, he was also faced with the cer-
tainty of death. In this state Bauby discovered what
he wanted to do more than anything.

I once went through a 48-hour period when I couldn't talk. I had a severe case of laryngitis, and my doctor forbade me to use my voice. It drove me crazy.

I thought about what would happen if I weren't able to communicate at all, to say the things I wanted to say. As I read Bauby's story, I was reminded of things I should say to my kids, but haven't—how proud I am of them, how much I love them, and how much I value them. I thought of my spouse, my friends, and my neighbors around me, and the words that I need to speak to them.

There was one part of Bauby's body that was able to move—his left eyelid. With a therapist he worked out an alphabet system whereby he would blink to confirm yes or no on the choice of an individual letter. Word by word he composed sentences in his mind and then dictated them one blink at a time.

His incredible book, the result of this painstaking dictation, has now been adapted as a film.

What Bauby wanted to do more than anything was communicate. And he chose to struggle to express himself with the last remaining muscle in his body. We never know when we may lose the ability to share our thoughts. From our first word to our last, we are given an incredible opportunity. Life is too short to let things go unsaid. Whatever the circumstance, we have the great power at our disposal to choose our words. Let's choose them wisely and then speak them while we can.

 RICK RUSAW

If you lost your ability to communicate, what words would you regret not saying to your family and friends? Take time to write some of those words down, and then plan to communicate them to your loved ones.
Write a prayer, asking God for the strength to speak the words that you need to say.

Do you often feel as if you don't have the right words to say? Set aside time to be still and listen for God's voice. Listen for the words that he wants to speak to you and that he wants you to speak to others. Write down what you hear.

Love one another deeply, from the heart.

1 PETER 1:22

Good Neighbors

Robert Frost, the dean of American poets, wrote these interesting words: "Good fences make good neighbors." What do you think he meant by that? I hear a bit of a defensive ring in this statement. In other words, build good fences, establish the boundaries, don't cross those boundaries and we'll get along just fine. Keep your grass trimmed, and I'll keep my hedges cut. I'll say "Good morning" to you and you can say "How are you?" back. If you send over cookies for the kids' birthdays, I'll send over a fruitcake for Christmas. We'll be "good neighbors." But is that really what a good neighbor looks like?

A long time ago a high-powered attorney asked Jesus what makes a good neighbor. The explanation Jesus gave was considerably different from Robert Frost's. Like he did so often, Jesus told a simple story (see Luke 10) as an answer to the question.

A man had been ambushed by thieves as he traveled a particular road. They took everything he had, beat him, and left him for dead. Shortly, a priest happened to come by and see the man, no doubt a rather arresting sight after having been beaten to a pulp. Not about to be tarnished by the nasty circumstances or the bloody mess, the priest crossed over to the other side of the road and walked on by. Not long after that, another religious leader came by and, remarkably, the same thing happened. He saw the beaten man in the road, suffering badly and destitute. What did he do? He walked on by.

And then a Samaritan, a man from a race of people despised in those days, saw the poor man in the road, stopped, knelt down, and helped him. He bandaged him, gave him some wine, picked him up, and took him to a little inn up the road. He then entrusted the owner of the inn, a complete stranger, with enough money to take care of the man until he was healthy. If there were additional expenses, he would be back to settle up. I'm assuming you'll find it rather easy to decide which one of the three was a good neighbor.

Leave it to Jesus to select a "bottom-feeder" for the main character of his story. We know this man only as a Samaritan. But that takes us somewhere very important toward the correct meaning of neighbor.

Because of his nationality we know this Samaritan was resented and held in contempt by just about everybody. He would be the very last person you and I would choose to illustrate anything!

Through the brilliance of his storytelling, Jesus had an inquiring attorney right where he wanted him. "So who was a neighbor to the man who fell into the hands of robbers?" Jesus asked. There was only one answer. "The one who had mercy on him," said the attorney. Oh, and there was one other thing Jesus said to the attorney. "Since you get it, now go do it."

Who are your neighbors (not just those who live near you, but also your coworkers, family, and fellow church members)? What needs are apparent in their lives?

Have you been stopping to help your neighbors who are hurting or in need, or have you been walking right by? Make a list of several ways that you will reach out to help your neighbors this week.